The Sun Is Hot
Inspirational Poetry

Michaela Sefler

PublishAmerica
Baltimore

ISBN: 1-4137-9003-8
PUBLISHED BY PUBLISHAMERICA, LLLP
www.publishamerica.com
Baltimore

Printed in the United States of America

To guiding lights....

TABLE OF CONTENTS

A DOOR

A door to open,
water to quench
a key to unlock
a window to free.
Open the door to a new horizon,
quench the thirst of thousands of years;
unlock a desire to rediscover
free ourselves from bondage and toil.
Yearning hearts,
inquiring minds,
wanting souls,
hungry lives.
Wanting mercy from a creator,
wanting forgiveness from above
asking for justice from a God,
asking for blessings from beyond.

AN ANCIENT ALTAR

An ancient altar remains;
a sacrifice from days of old,
an oath to last the ages
a faith unshaken and true.
As strong as steel
as deep as the oceans
as true as belief
as eternal as love.
An altar where his faith lies
an altar where his resolve is laid
a sacrifice where his hope is harnessed
a sacrifice where his fears are bared.
A faith he steadily nurtures
a faith he eternally knows
an oath he swore to keep
an oath that penetrates the ages.
The earth was shaken
the sky broke up
the winds were whaling
for their honor.
An altar, a sacrifice
upon which they weep,
an oath a belief
upon which they worship.

MERCY AND JUDGMENT

Mercy and judgment,
interplay of truth.
Glory and victory,
interplay of triumph.
Chivalry and bravery,
manifestations of prevalence.
Building a kingdom,
conquering a land,
laying out a foundation,
sketching a plan.
Establishing a throne,
creating a dream,
kingdoms and crowns,
forever a city.
An establishment, a faith
for eternity.
Two faces facing each other
for harmony.
Thrones of glory,
thrones of fate,
thrones of majesty
opening the gates.

ONLY TRUTH

Only truth can withstand the times,
forever a promise, forever a vow
Only true love can withstand the tides,
forever a life, forever a dream
Only with faith can we overcome
unchanging realities, unchanging facts
Only with faith can we ever hope
to receive our portion, receive our call
Only with integrity can we ever hope
to receive an inheritance from above
Only with honor can we ever return
to a state as intended, faithful and true
Only with searching and wanting hearts
can we ever hope to receive our law
Only with faithfulness
can we hope to overcome
Only with stubbornness and everlasting quests
can we ever hope to see a sign
Only with unshaken resolve
can we ever hope to see the light

A CANDLE TO LIGHT

A candle to light,
a garment to clothe,
a lamp to aluminate,
a tent to warm.
Barefoot and naked,
waiting for right,
pleading for answers,
shivering with fright.
A candle to illuminate,
a lantern to light,
a ray to lighten,
a day to brighten.
A garment to clothe,
a house to shelter,
a boat to transport,
a ferry to carry.
Cold and weary
hoping for a hand
praying for salvation
pleading for mercy.

AN ANCIENT LIGHT

An ancient light sustaining us,
an ancient light encouraging us,
helping us endure,
helping us understand.
Rays and pillars worlds away,
coming and going, touching our ways
forever a promise
forever strong.
The sounds are the same
and so is the promise
finishing sentences
from long ago.
Ancient light
shining down
ancient light
coming through.
Supporting the moment
where we surely fainted
holding us strong
when we surely collapsed.
Continuing our sentences
finishing our words
completing a cycle
letting us turn.
Letting the world
turn on its axis
letting the world
develop as planned.

BEAUTY FORGIVES

Beauty forgives
kindness forgets
love lets go
gentleness lets be.
Streams wash the earth
water flows
tides break
rivers wash.
Remember my dreams
remember my fears
remember my hopes
remember my tears.
Only God's mercy will let
only faith will heal
only prayer will summon
only pleading will bring forgiveness.
Beauty forgives
kindness forgets
love lets go
gentleness lets be.

A TRUTH CALLS OUT

A truth calls out
from days of old
penetrating our hearts
this very day, to last the ages.
There are few differences
in this vast existence
from those ancient days,
from long ago.
We continue our lives
trying to connect
to that old connection
that can only illuminate.
Illuminate our existence
our fears
our presence
our tears.
I wouldn't want to cross the line
I wouldn't want to pass the oath.
So many words taken for granted
so many promises made in vain.
Tell me the difference between
conformity and truth
tell me the difference between
excess and enough.
Those ancient days
where the blueprint was impressed
live in our hearts
this very day.
Established then
for eternity;
upheld in our minds
forever.

I wouldn't want to err
or confuse what is right.
So many wonders ignored
so many gifts detained.
Tell me what counts as real
tell me what is prudence and truth
tell me what is greed
tell me what is love.

MY PAIN SO STRONG

My need is so great
that you come running
my need is so deep
that you come asking.
My pain is so strong
you are the one crying
my pain resounds
you are the one fighting.
My wounds are so deep
you wail in pain
my wounds are so deep
you scream in fright.
Let me leave
so I can rest my bones
let me leave
so I can heal my soul.

A VISION I KEEP

A vision I keep
of equity and fairness,
a dream I harbor
of truth and honor.
Simple lines, simple responses;
faithful words spoken on time.
An ambition I keep
of excellence.
A plan, a way
I remember
laid from days of old.
Simple blocks, simple desires
spoken and actualized in simplicity.
A faith, a religion kept for the ages
by luminous souls, great figures.
A belief, an inheritance held close
by great minds, faithful servants.
Wise sayings, mystical verses
written urgently by thirsty souls.
A difficult road, complex instruction
given by a living God
worshipped and learned over the ages
by the faithful men.
A religion to last, a covenant that stood
handed down with confidence
books written down, a way of life given
cherished and learned by the studious mind.
Old texts and ancient books stored away
read with awe for eternity
Prayers and hopes rise to the heavens,
waiting to be answered.

MEN OF GLORY

Merchants and sailors
men of God
travelers and shepards
men of glory.
Setting out on their journey
to face their fate
setting out to the stormy sea
awakening with the rising sun.
Going out into the wilderness
venturing into the night
never forgetting their visions of truth
never forgetting their rights.
Pleading to an eternal God
keeping an ancient oath
remembering eternal vows
living an eternal life.
The boats have sailed to sea
promised to return,
on board dreams and hopes
colors and ropes.
Eager minds wait
hopeful hearts yearn
lonley souls pray
for their return.
These men who knowingly nod
who seem to know of worlds beyond
these men whose hearts are filled with hope
who know peace, who know faith.

FOR BEAUTY I WAIT

For beauty I wait
for my portion I hope
for eternity I pray
for ideals I see.
I wait for a beauty within
I wait for a true existence
I wait for my inheritance
I wait for the promised land.
I hope you won't ignore me
I hope you won't set me aside
I hope you will consider my dreams
I hope you won't disregard my rights.
I live for an eternal promise
I live for an eternal dream
I live for a covenant from old
I strive for an existence from above.

TWELVE ROADS

Twelve tribes reign
twelve blessings bestowed
twelve flags to represent
twelve roads to journey.
A bow and arrow,
scales of justice.
a boat with sails
symbols in our times.
The sun and moon
wheat of the fields
a house of God
for eternity.
The signs from heaven
an all encompassing love
bounty and victory
instruction from above.
Handed down for the ages
a dawn, a rising sun
as dew in the morning light
as a stream in a dying land.
Lions to rule
troops to reign
wolves to roam the land
a whelp to hide.
Wells to quench
streams to subdue
a thirst from within
a desire for truth.
Given as a map,
given as a code
signs of guidance
signs of hope.

HEROIC FIGURES

Those heroic figures
that stood long ago,
their ancient souls'voices
resound to this day.
They upheld our honor
upheld our peace
they kept our strength,
kept our dreams.
Those forgiving souls
that lived long ago
resound in our hearts,
resound in our hopes.
Upholding our desires
our dreams and our lives,
upholding our ideals.
The world won't budge
the world won't turn
without these souls
willing us on.
Every breath is a moment later,
every change a building block;
every turn reconciles.
no words or phrases
can deny these structures
that bind our world together;
can't deny these pillars
that keep our faith alive.
Suspending truths, suspending legends
holding time and immortality,
souls suspend a faltering world,
building our hopes for eternity.

AT THE POINT OF NOTHING

In the world where nothing happens,
at the point where nothing gets done
that is where you expect me
that is when you run.
To draw water from a rock,
to be satiated in the heat of the desert
to see in the fog of day
to rejoice in the longest hour.
In the world where nothing ever happens
at the point of giving up
that is where you want me
that is when you are.
You compete with my senses
you want to beat my mind
you want to find out in seconds
what can take a lifetime.
There is a miracle you must believe in
the impossible, you have faith in
bringing light from darkness,
turning water into wine.

AN ACTUAL LOSS

A current injustice
an actual loss
a real story
a true tale.
I fight with my own honor
I fight with my own name
I fight with my own justice
I fight with my own pain.
I toiled for myself
I let you be,
I suffered for our difference
I let you see.
I left you in peace
I came when you asked
I let you thrive
I let you try.
My own inheritence
on the front lines,
my own winnings
displayed for nothing.
My own pain, my own injustice
my life played out so the world can see
my losses sold, my winnings portrayed
my talent wasted.

LIGHTS

Angels from heaven
stars shining through
lights dancing eternally
beams of hope getting in.
Angels accompanying
stars complementing
lights brightening
pillars supporting.
Angels keep our blessings
stars glorify the heavens
lighting the crowns of the creator
stones wanting to build.
To build a city so glorious,
to keep an existence strong
to guard a faltering life
to uphold a promise so deep.
Angels who never sleep
ride chariots through the heavens.
Princes reign the earth;
God oversees our chances.

TODAY I SIT IN THE SHADE

Today I sit in the shade
while you run for your life,
today I sit in the shade
while you say it is surely over.
Today I rest my head
while you speak of your fading dreams,
Today I sit in the shade
you say it won't be back.
Today I sit in the shade
while you run frantic,
Today I sit in the shade
while you run wild.
Today I sit in the shade
the day that it is over,
today I rest my head
and you said I was dead.
Today I sit in the shade
and your ploys are for naught,
today I sit in the shade
the day I was supposed to cry.
You said I was not
you said I would suffer
you said I was unworthy
you said I could cry.

I SAW THE WORLD

I saw the world come and go
that is why I stand today;
I saw the world go up and fall
that is why my heart still mourns.
I saw the world go up in smoke
that is why I can still cry;
I saw the world crash to the ground
that is why I can still plead.
I saw the world beg for hope
that is why I can still pray;
I saw the world hope for peace
that is why I can still live.

GESTURES AND TOKENS

I learned to walk,
I learned to smile,
I learned to try,
I learned to cry.
I learned to sweat,
I learned to work,
I learned to feel,
I learned to cope.
Yet gestures and tokens
are what I got;
gestures and tokens
are all you meant.
I won the war,
I won the race;
I overcame failure,
I overcame pain.
I conquered my fears,
mourned my losses
I faced my daemons
felt my tears.
Yet gestures and tokens
is what you gave me
gestures and tokens
is all you have.

A CHARIOT

A chariot from heaven
is transcribed on earth;
a kingdom reins
in our universe.
By wisdom and understanding
the streets are ruled,
by wisdom and understanding
mercy is bestowed.
By brave acts and victorious merit
the world is conquered
by brave acts and victorious merit
the quest is glorious.
Beauty lives in the heart of perfection
beauty lives in a perfect union
foundations are laid in the heart of toil
foundations are laid with a faith that is strong.
A kingdom is erected
after much judgment
a crown is placed
on the head of a king.

CLOTHE MY SOUL

Clothe my soul
give me form
let me shine
let me learn.
A candle, a light
to brighten the night
a beacon a sign
illuminating a right.
Clothe my soul
warm my bones
give me rights
desire my world.
Light my way,
illuminate my night,
release these never-ending questions,
never-ending doubts.
Weariness and hunger
deprivation and neglect
are conditions of humanity
a condition of regret.

ANGELS RETURNING

Angels returning
from a world above
have witnessed
the glory from beyond.
Angels returning from a journey
long and weary
are graced by the beauty
of the heavens above.
Angels overseeing a fragile existence
know we count
Angels guarding our tiresome steps
know that we can overcome.
Coming and going,
they hold our chances
descending and ascending;
supporting our fall.

ALWAYS GLORIOUS

So glorious, so true
so perfect so real
paved in gold
a winning cup.
Will you make it through?
Will you prevail?
Will you win your rights?
Will you make the cut?
Always glorious
always true
always majestic
but will you make it through?
Who will live?
Who will try?
Who will surrender?
Who will actualize?
It was glorious,
it was right
the ultimate road,
the ultimate right.
It's the last time you fail,
the last time you cry
the last time you pay
for someone else's right.

DON'T FORGET

My weakness might let you in
my instability lets you off the hook,
but don't forget I am willing to stand
don't forget I am willing to stay.
I am ready to stand
and ask for justice
I am ready to stay
and let you feel my soul.
My oversight might let you forget,
my delinquency might let you pass,
but don't forget I am ready to sit
and ready to hear what needs to be said.
 I am ready to sit
until the whole truth is honored
I am ready to hear
all that is told.
My forgetfulness might open the door
my clumsiness might let you get away
but don't forget I want to be heard
don't forget I want to be judged.
 I am ready to talk
and let them hear my story
I am ready to plead
and ask for my rights.
My heart is open
my body can bear
my cup is empty
my children are there.
I am ready to stand
and ask for justice
I am ready to stay
and let you feel my heart.

I SAW YOU LAST NIGHT

I saw you last night,
your face so bright,
you said it was nothing
you acted so right.
I saw you last night,
as though I was dreaming,
I saw you last night
confident and true.
You said it was nothing,
  you acted so lightly,
you said you were fine
nothing to lose.
Strength is your silence
your loss,
your endurance,
your truth.

IT WILL CORRODE MY BONES

I was awakened by a moment
of nothingness
a moment of fear
a moment of darkness a moment of tears.
It will corrode my bones if I give up,
it will eat my pride if I forget.
My heart will falter if I let go,
my integrity will die if I walk away.
I will keep my strength
to remain clear-headed
I will keep my sense of justice,
to remain in peace.
Don't tell me no lies
or toy with my heart;
don't tamper with my intelligence,
don't betray my night.
I'll stand strong
I'll wait 'til the end
I'll endure the hardship
and I will make a stand.
It will corrode my bones if I give in,
and eat away my pride if I let go.
My heart will falter if I forget what counts
my integrity will die if I forget what is right.

YOUR OWN PLIGHT

Your own road
your own destiny
your own word in print
your own life.

Your own plight,
your own tears,
your own lessons
your own fears.
Remember your roots
remember your lashes,
remember your honor,
remember your shame.
You must know the difference
between right and wrong
know the difference
between dignity and shame.
Know the difference,
know the score,
know your suffering,
know the wrongs.
Storm or clear weather
you must wait for an answer
dark sky and silence
worship and consent.

A MIRACLE

When my will surpasses
your actions;
when my will surpasses
your truth;
when my love surpasses
justice
when my love surpasses
pain.
A miracle will surely happen
a miracle will appear
I will find water
for my thirsty will.
When my favor surpasses
your charity
when my honor surpasses
your cruelty
when my graciousness overrules
the injustice,
when nature overides
your corrosion.
A miracle will surely happen,
a miracle will surely appear
I will find mercy
in this final year.

LET ME BEAR MY RIGHT

My pain is mine
my suffering is part of me
don't take it away
you'll break my heart.
Let me bear my rights,
let me bear my hopes
let me bear my dreams
let my bear my loss.
Otherwise I am nothing
not worthy of a cause
otherwise I am worthless
not worthy of a right.
I must live my life,
learn my lessons,
feel my attributes,
receive my law.
I will plead for justice,
plead for a listening ear
I will pray for my existence,
pray for my will.

LISTEN TO THE TIMES

Walk with the days,
listen to the times,
feel the winds,
know the tides.
Listen to the wisdom,
listen to the rhymes,
listen to the storm,
listen to the calm.
Walk with strangers,
walk with friends,
talk to people,
see their ways.
Every rustling tree
every flowing stream
every speaking tongue
every rising sun.
Listen to the times,
walk with the days,
these are given
these are the rays.
Heed to my Voice,
look with caring eyes,
listen to the world,
know what is right.
Listen to the times,
walk with the days,
listen to the winds,
learn the ways.
Actuality before you,
truth in front of your eyes,
learn to decipher,
learn to try.

NOTHING BUT HOPE

I have nothing but my hope,
nothing but my dreams;
I have nothing but my desire,
nothing but my ideals.
My hope is to live
my dream is to be
my desire is to prevail
my ideals are to be free.
I am poor and broken,
you are in dire straights
I am down cast and weary
and you can't get it straight.
You are no longer listening
and I can barely hear;
I am no longer in tune
but you are no longer here.
I have nothing but my loss,
I have nothing but my tears;
I have nothing but this chance,
nothing but these years.

VICTORY

Judgment and forgiveness,
severity and mercy,
victory and bravery,
kingship and foundation.
A pillar is justice that gives rise to mercy
a pillar is justice that gives rise to forgiveness.
Victory arises from bravery
a kingdom is build from a solid foundation.
Wisdom and understanding
are the crowns of creation.
Beauty is the glory of perfection,
Knowledge is a building block.
Bravery arises from
fairness and belief.
Glory arises
from a brave victory.
Creation is born from a perfect Kingdom
ruled and reigned by a living God,
ministered by wisdom and understanding
which bestow justice and mercy.

BECAUSE I STILL DO

Because I still love you
that your beauty is still
because I still think about you
that your chance is well
Because I won't forget
my vows and promises
that your voice
is heard.
Because I won't forget
my visions and hopes
that your desire
is felt.
Because I still stand
in your broken promise
that all can hear
your fading voice.
Because I won't forget
my oath and vows
that you can still feel
in the cold of night.
Because I cannot forget
my calling and promise
that I must lend an ear
in this wasted land.
I still hear your voice
I still feel your heart
I hear your pleas
in the dark of night.

DEFLECTED

My life is deflected into a thousand rays,
my dreams are scattered in a hundred ways,
my hopes are shattered to the ground
my desires are reflected in the wind.
Deflected into the morning sun,
I am like a rainbow in the sky,
scattered through the hopes of time,
like dust in the wind.
Asking for a steady hand,
asking for another chance,
asking for knowing soul
to help me make a stand.
I must make a stand and gather my losses,
make a stand and endure the time,
make a stand and regroup my chances,
make a stand and rearrange my right.
I will gather a broken collective
I will endure an irreconcilable result;
I will reunite a faltering existence
to rearrange a scattered world.
I see scattered remnants of a world,
scattered pillars of an old religion,
scattered aspects of a whole,
scattered rays of an everlasting hope.
Deflections and reflections
of reality,
prayers and pleas
for a living truth.

FOR GENERATIONS I WAITED

For generations I waited,
over the years I prayed,
a thousand years and more,
I toiled for your grace.
I built a kingdom thoughtfully,
waited on an existence so pure;
I lifted the hopes of many
and kept the faith of more.
I cried for your future,
cried for your loss
cried for your hour,
cried for your morn.
I built towers made of stone,
created a city to last the ages,
planned an existence carefully,
foresaw a life for generations.
I planted a field,
tilled a garden
nurtured an orchard
fed a world.

I CAN STILL REMEMBER

I remember your quest
I remember your dreams
I remember your endurance
I remember your fears.
You endured a battle for integrity,
you fought for stability,
a quest for a higher ground,
and an undying commitment to eternity.
I remember what you counted on
I remember what you feared
I remember your dreams,
commitments and tears.
It will actualize
if we can only remember
it will come true
if we can only believe.
I remember your right
to higher existence
I remember your commitment
to a true understanding.
Will it be true?
if we can only remember
what will actualize?
If we truly heed.
I can still feel your desires
I can still feel your hopes
I can still remember your plight
I can still remember your loss.
I would be a fool to forget
your fading dreams
the ones
that might still take form.

I would be a fool to forget
I would be a fool to disregard you
I would be a fool to continue
without your love.
You won't forget
or let go
those old promises
that still remind.
They remind you of a better existence,
remind you of a higher love,
remind you of an old promise
that was given to you for surety.
Your stubborn stance, won't let you forget
your truthfulness won't let you take it for granted
your loyalty has surpassed
my infidelity by miles and miles.

I MISSED YOUR VOICE

I missed your voice
in the hearts of the young,
I missed your eyes
in the spectators and crowds.
I missed your face,
in eager smiles,
I missed your style,
in the evening crowds.
I missed your whisper
in the streams and rivers
I missed your calling
in the mountain echoes.
When will you return?
when will you bestow?
your eternal blessing
and eternal call.

I WAS OUT THE DOOR

I was out the door
sure it was over
my bags were packed
long ago.
I turned my head
you were still talking
I turned my head
and heard your voice.
Something about love and honor
perfect justice and eternity
peace and freedom
plans to redeem.
I turned my head;
I thought I was dreaming
you said everything that was in my dreams;
your voice resounded,
over the hills.
You spoke of forgiveness
and fading dreams
you spoke of redemption
and forgotten tears.
I thought I was dreaming
hearing your voice
resounding through
the universe.

ON THE HORIZON

On the horizon I saw your face,
in the sunset I saw your hope,
In the dark of night I perceived your visions.
In the light of day I perceived your dreams.
Ahead of the times,
ahead of the plans,
ahead of the expectation,
ahead of the rhymes.
A life as sweet
as my greatest desire
a life as right
as my favorite dream.
I saw visions of life as intended
visions of life as planned;
I remembered my promise,
remembered my hopes.
I saw your hope
in the fading horizon;
I saw your aspirations
on the resting moon.
Like a storm in the heart of the ocean
like a storm in the desert land
will you rise like a phoenix?
will you set like the sun?

THE BELLS RANG

The bells rang and
children screamed;
orphans wept
and hungry hearts cried.
The bells rang to foretell
pleaded for existence,
asked for mercy,
screamed to be heard.
God did enough.
when he created the heavens
God did enough
when he created the earth.
We still have the freedom to choose
our actions;
the freedom to change
a failing plan;
the freedom to create
a better existence;
the freedom to forgive
faltering lives.

THE DANCERS DANCED

The dancers danced,
the singers sang,
the lovers yearned,
the mourners cried.
The kings foretold
and the princes wept;
the ministers advised
and the queens looked on.
On terraces they hovered
on fountains they wept
on doorsteps they waited
on castle gates they hoped.
They hoped for a changing existence,
hoped for a progressing plan,
hoped for a new direction
hoped for a final run.

TOWERS AND CITIES

Towers and cities
in darkness
they stand.
Fortresses and walls
in shadows
they watch.
Castles and gates
in wilderness
they keep.
Angels and chariots
in heavens
they roam.
Blessings and gifts
on earth
are bestowed.

WHAT AM I?

What am I, if you are not?
what am I,if you are gone?
what am I,if you are right?
what am I,if I am wrong?
What am I, if my truth is wanting?
what am I, if your truth is whole?
what am I,if I already understand?
what am I, if you already know?.
What am I, if I can't have you?
what am I, if you are the only one?
what am I, if my world is wanting?
what am I, if your world is right?

WHEN I SAW YOU FALL

When I saw you fall,
my heart trembled;
when I saw you lose,
my heart cried.
When I saw you falter
my fists clenched;
when I saw you shatter,
my eyes burnt.
In the morning
I felt your hopes;
in the morning,
I felt your dreams.
I remembered how you tried to sustain,
a failing existence
I remembered how you tried to sustain,
a failing chance.

YOU STAYED
THROUGH THE NIGHT

Yesterday I heard your voice,
yesterday I heard you whisper.
I heard your footsteps,
I heard you cry.
Your voice reminded me
of my blessing;
your voice reminded me
of my chance.
You comforted my trying heart,
you held me in my failing stance,
you touched my hair
and said I was right.
You wiped off the tears
and told me to stand
you brushed my hair,
told me to try.
You stayed through the night
until I knew;
you stayed 'til dawn
when the sun came through.

ONE WOMAN

One woman left the game,
one woman took the hand,
one woman wants it all,
one woman wants it right.
One woman saw deception,
one woman saw opportunity,
one woman saw suffering,
one woman took her chance.
One woman unable to pass,
one woman walked all night,
one woman cried for more,
one woman said it was enough.
One woman said he was hers,
one woman knelt in fright,
one woman urges us on,
one woman begs for her right.

IN THE CASTLES OF JUDAH

In the castles of David
did I recall your name;
in the castles of Judah
did I learn of your fame.
In the castles of Solomon
did I learn to know
in the castles of glory;
did I learn to sow.
Days passed long ago,
justice and hope
spills over for eternity.
In the hills of Jerusalem
did I breath so deep;
In the chambers of kings
did I so soundly sleep.
In the hearts of princes
did I begin to talk
in the hearts of kings
did I learn to love.

A WORD WILL INSPIRE

A word will inspire,
a sentiment will cure,
a verse will uplift,
truth can change.
Another moment,
another step,
another chance,
another hope.
A rhyme can know,
a story can tell,
a feeling change,
a thought transforms.
Another turn,
another life,
another cycle,
another prayer.

MERCY IS LIGHT

Mercy is light,
in discipline we learn,
in beauty we strive,
for excellence to see.
Brave is your quest
for higher ground;
winnings are yours
in fertility.
Together we climb
to a higher existence
blessings are here
in abundance and bounty.
Step by step
we grow together,
to worship a God,
to know ourselves.

CONDITION

The state of the world
the state of our progress
the condition of humanity
the condition of our plights.
Day after day,
night after night,
legends are told;
for freedom we fight.
Elevate us from apathy;
summon mercy from above,
raise our hopes towards another day
raise our sights to higher ground.

TO BE THE FIRST

To be the first to overcome,
to be the first to bring an offering,
to be the first to hope,
the first to rise.
To be the first after the storm,
the first after the breaking,
the first after the loss,
the first after the reckoning.
To be the first is the right of excellence,
the right enlightenment,
the right of the chosen,
the right of the light.

ALL WATERS RETURN

All waters return,
all answers arrive.
Rivers flow;
rains fall down.
All children hear
the whispers in the night.
All people know
their lacks and wants.
Possessions forgotten
return again;
memories set aside
once again awaken.
One maker
keeps them together,
One God
will guarantee.

PASSAGE

Timelessness
hearts mend.
Timelessness
love is remembered.
Passing through a passage
dark as the night
passing through a tunnel
long as the fight.
Timelessness
the waves have calmed.
Timelessness
the storms have passed.
Reaching the shorelines,
with freedom to reap,
seeing a lighthouse,
they forget servitude and sleep.
Awakenings
from a forever sleep.
Awakenings
into the hope of the ages.
Ancient beginnings
repeat perpetually,
remind and resemble
days from antiquity.
Awakenings
from a slumber.
Awakenings
towards dreams and redemption.
I walked along the highways
through times and worlds
I walked along the rooftops
of cities and ancient ruins.

ONE GOD

There is one God up in the heavens
faithful and real;
one God up in the heavens
terrible and true.
You can cry,
you can hide
but there is One God up in the heaven
garbed in majesty and
adorned with signs.
There are signs that govern,
days that guide,
elements that rule,
over our times;
placed under the heavens
placed under stars
placed before lives
placed before the times.
One God up in the heavens
leting us know,
we learn to hear,
learn to follow
He is the maker, the ruler, the One.

AWAIT IN RUINS

Civilizations await in ruins,
recalling an eternal plan
cities await in hope
recalling a perfect promise.
We receive instruction and wisdom
through the times
we forget the silence
of long ago teachings.
All eyes look up to answer
all minds recall the light
all hearts anticipate
all souls acknowledge the night.
Who will answer?
who will know?
who will rise?
who will fall?
Another night,
another day
unfold
in anticipation.

I WILL NEVER
STOP BELIEVING

I will never stop believing
that my promise is still.
I will never stop believing
that my failures will be redeemed.
I lived a life
before I knew you
I left a life
before I saw.
I left a truth
that meant the world to me.
I left a love
before I knew,
I will never stop believing,
that my life is still
I will never stop believing
that my life is real.
Don't draw me in
ot take me back
to an endless whirlwind
of never-ending doubt.

STILL INNOCENT

Freedom is pure,
desire is innocent;
don't confuse their ways
don't touch their right.
I believe in a love from ancient times,
a destiny written,
a hope from long ago,
a question already answered.
Beginnings from the millennium
are humbly resolved.
Beginnings from creation
are quietly answered.
Still innocent,
hoping to find a way
still innocent
transforming days.
Changing hearts,
winning souls,
bring peace
bring joy.
Don't oppress freedoms
don't darken paths
a soul still illuminates
a light still shines.

THE VERY MOMENT

He battled
for his honor,
he battled
for his name.
He fought for his own recall
he yearned for his own longing.
He gave up his honor
for a sin he did not know.
He struggled eternally
to keep up a moment,
the one that let him cry
and let him feel his fright.
That very moment,
made him an equal
that very moment,
broke him down.
The moment he saw,
the moment he came
he knew he would never lose again,
he knew he would never win.
The very moment he conquered,
the very moment he achieved,
he knew he would never surrender;
he knew of his imperfect state.
That very moment he battled,
that very moment he fought;
he knew it was forever
he knew it was the end.

INSIGNIFICANT

My own insignificance
my own pain
my own failure
my own shame.
Your own weaknesses
must you know
your own nothingness
must you feel.
Insignificant,
humble before you
nothingness
modest and true.
Cry
return
forgive
mourn.

YOUR VIRTUE STILL WAITS

Your fears keep you alive,
your blindness is your innocence
your surety makes you vulnerable,
your oaths guard the night.
How will you know?
How will you grow?
How will you see?
How will you be?
Your virtue still waits,
your fears were appeased,
your reluctance won the race,
yet your jealousy burned it all.
Will you win?
Will you master?
Will you know?
Will you deserve?.

A GUIDING LIGHT

A guiding light shines
upon a windy street
a guiding light shines
amid the ruins.
Surrender into the night
in spite of darkness;
surrender unto the times
in spite of stormy waters.
Upon the confusion and fear
I felt adamant reproof;
upon the noisy streets
I saw a guiding light.
Instruction and wisdom
call me back.
I remember that the hurt
will show me the way.
Long ago fortunes
blown in the wind;
long ago fortunes
echo in the night.
Slight recall
will remember;
elusive wonder
will bring back lives.

CONQUERED AT LAST

Fury and storms,
jealousy and fire
will consume
until mercy is summoned.
Hope and prosperity
love and counsel
will heal
until all returns.
Confusion and terror
loss and delusion
will strike
when all do mourn.
On winding streets I lived,
I hid;
on narrow paths
I fought and battled
on empty roads betrayed and wounded.
On arduous ways I conquered at last.

A RESPONSE

I seek a response, an attempt
a question in due time.
I seek a step, in touch
with the beats of the night.
I waited in silence
for a decent response
to let me stand
or at least attempt.
I attempted to voice
an enduring truth,
attempted to come closer
to an only chance.
Lines connect,
memory recalls,
echoes remember,
rays filter through.
Remanants of a life
surrender to a higher existence;
while the forgiveness of derision,
is lost time.

TO STRIVE

To strive, to conquer,
to inquire, to learn,
to thirst, to receive,
to want, to become.
Higher callings,
set and sure
higher striving
faithful and true.
To desire, to honor,
to dream, to fulfill,
to love, to yearn,
to hear, to see.
I am standing for a moment
on solid ground
urging promises,
remembered in time.

IN A WORLD OF GHOSTS

In a world of ghosts
where saviors were forgotten
I will remember you
so you can be.
In a world of heroes
where saviors are upheld
surely fortune is in abundance,
in the land that is remembered.
In a world of ghosts
where salvation has passed by
weakness will reign,
sin will be looked upon.
In a world of heroes
where redemption has been awaited
blessings will come through,
sin will be transformed.

IN CAPTIVITY I WAIT

In captivity I wait;
your gates I must open,
your temple walls
will protect my ground.
Protect me from the lashings
of existence;
protect me from the drunkenness
of the times.
Your sacrifices
will melt the oppression;
the ropes that bind me
will come undone.
The chains that hold me will burn
because of your pleas;
cruelty will dissipate
because of your righteousness.
In captivity I wait;
your gates I must open,
your temple walls
will let me overcome.

IN MAJESTIC HALLS

In majestic halls of heavenly abodes
where wine overflows in sanctity,
you wait in grace and patience
for my offering.
On golden paths
of hope and glory
you humbly await
my rising sun.
I pray to heed;
I pray to listen
to your calling
of higher love.
Feed my soul
so I don't falter;
feed my will
so I don't stray.
In glorious castles you await
to see my fleeting grace,
so you can bless once more,
my hopes and prayers.
In your sanctuary you abide
to feel that remnant chance
that your name can be praised and rooted
in fertile ground to grow.
In chambers of glory,
on wings of angels you do stand,
watching in hope, this arduous existence;
perhaps another chance will plant.
On the rays of the sun
you look down on me
to see perhaps that I will too
speak of your eternity.

I WAIT

I wait for Your graciousness
to feel my lowly stance,
so I can perhaps uphold
even for a moment told.
Perhaps this time
You will answer finally
my broken state,
my humble plea.
Another turn
will be decided
another portion
will be inherited.
I hope this time
our voice will waken
the people's slumber
of apathy.

HIS SANCTUARY HOLDS

His face is clear,
his countenance shines
his manners are well,
his body is strong.
He watched his loss,
devastated,
yet wholesome;
his heart awaits.
His sanctuary holds
his guardians alive;
his sanctuary holds
his hope true.
His priests minister
a sanctuary
from ancient times;
they worship an altar
from days of old.
His times withstand
a loss greater then all;
his steps carry
the burden of the generations.
His shoulders are strong
his back supports,
his hands still form
the expectations of his Lord.
His time carries
the loss of existence;
his time mends
broken hearts.
Still withstanding
the whims of creation
still carrying
the burdens of the times.

TO TRANSFORM

He will transform humanity,
bring the people to higher planes
he will educate the masses,
bring salvation from within.
He will show the glory
and transform the pain;
he will lift the people
to praise his God.
He is strong and sure
steadfast and everlasting
in victorious merits
of nobility.

CLUTCHING HER SON

Clutching her son,
she watches as he is leaving.
Holding her baby
she weeps as he walks out the door.
He wonders how this ever happened,
he wonders how she let him go;
he wonders how she survived,
he wonders how she still recalls.
Clutching her son
she gives him her blessing;
holding her baby
she lets him get away.
He wonders how he can change,
he wonders how she can know
he wonders how he can rectify
a loss he doesn't even remember.

MY LIFE CAN COMFORT

My life can comfort
that everlasting right;
my sacrifice will surely endure
the debt of your life.
My broken state can surely aid
your vast eternal existence;
my strength can surely lift
your sorrows and your pains.
My tears will surely reach
and melt the hardness of the times;
my wounds will surely call out
to the ears of the land.
Don't set me aside,
don't forget me;
I must have lived for something.
Surely I can count.
If I die tonight
without a chance
bury me
so I can be forgotten.

IN YOUR PALACE

In your palace,
your abode,
you wait in mercy
to respond.
to a multitude of pleas,
a myriads of processions;
you wait humbly to hear
who will finally will heed.
Don't let me fall.
Don't let me fail.
Don't trample my offering,
don't hide my sacrifice.
Listen to my voice and
hear my desperation;
my pleas must be heard,
my wounds must be tended.

MASTER OF THE WORLD

How can it be,
master of the universe,
I reached the end
of all my worlds?
How can it be
that my desire fails
when I have ventured
all highways left?
How can you turn me away
this last time
I already told you
all.
How can it be
that my want is lacking
when I already traveled
all roads before me?
How can you turn me away?
this time
it is clear
that I am nothing.
Are all my pleas
be for naught,
are all my efforts
blown in the wind?
Please give me Your steady hand,
please see me through this darkest day;
so I can hearken this last time,
so your servant is not turned away.

HEARD YOUR PLEAS

I heard you calling,
heard your pleas
as though forsaken
when you cried.
I reassured you
that the ties that bind
will stand today;
the doubts and failures
will fade away.
I heard you calling,
felt your fears;
I cried for your failings,
cried for your tears.
I blessed your voice,
blessed your name;
I hope you will answer
and believe my fame.
I watch the heavens,
I watch the earth,
to see you rise
and make a stand.
I will wait forever
for glory and truth;
I will wait forever
for the Glory of you.

AFTER THE WAR

I came back after the war,
your eyes unchanged, your voice assured.
You said nothing can ruin your stay,
nothing can spoil your chances.
I wanted so much
to believe in your voice;
I hoped this time would be the last
that we would endure this destruction.
Reassured by your clear eyes
reassured by your softness,
reassured by your answers,
reassured by your surety.
You will win,
you will wait,
you will persevere,
if only I can wait.
You were unshaken even in my desperation;
you gave me strength when all was lost.
you stood your ground when all was wasted,
never will you falter, never will you fail.

AUSPICIOUS NIGHT

The winds blew all night,
that night that you walked in.
The clouds drew in hastily
as though in anger.
Your gift overshadows me,
yet the night falls eagerly.
Your fortunes are great,
yet shadows hover.
Your eloquence is captivating,
yet the winds still wail.
Your virtue is great
yet pain still lingers.
The moon is bright
in this auspicious night;
it reflects your beauty
and tolerance.
Your greatness is adored,
your greatness is upheld
your sovereignity
still wins, by worlds away.

YOUR LETTERS AND SIGNS

There are only a few
that speak of Your Glory,
only a few
that still recount.
A few tie
Your letters and signs;
a few recount
those lessons from old.
A few cry enough
to feel;
a few vow
and carry the promise.
Their oaths mend
broken vessels,
their lives endure
a broken existence.
Their promises prevail
and even carry
the hopes for glory
and virtuous truth.
Bringing back
what was once shattered,
believing and returning
what was once lost.

DESIRES, WANTS AND HOPES

Desires, wants and hopes,
yearnings and sacrifice
effort and toil
that is truth and reality.
Desires to become
desires to feel
desires be
desires to prevail.
Wanting to learn
wanting to grow
wanting to know
wanting to see.
Hope to become
hope to excel
hope to overcome
hope to achieve.
Yearnings for a union
yearnings for transcendence
yearning to arrive
yearnings for love.
Investing time,
sacrificing love,
sacrificing effort,
sacrificing tolerance,
sacrificing fortunes.

UPHOLD AND BELIEVE

The difference lies
in his hope,
the difference lies
in his prayer;
the difference lies
in his belief,
the difference
lies in his destiny.
His future is blessed
and virtuously upheld
because he faithfully
believes it.
A covenant he made
to uphold and believe,
a covenant he keeps
of his glory and fame.
He believes and upholds
promises and fortunes;
he believes and upholds
actualities and ends.

EARTH UNSHAKEN

Earth unshaken,
might so strong,
unmoved promises
in peace are bound.
Bravery is rooted,
challenges are taken,
promises are remembered
swords are drawn.
Legends are told,
eternity is spoken,
victory is attempted,
sovereignity is reached.
Wars are conquered,
established at last;
forgotten vows
and duels unfold.
An eternity,
of my desires;
seeking protection
of an eternal God.

I WILL WAIT

A prisoner
to your name,
for your ideals
I must wait.
A prisoner,
yet blessed
your actualization
I ponder.
I will appease
Your desire.
In jealousy
you might wonder.
To summon your truth
will keep my name;
only to know
of Your glory.
The highest of truths
will free my doubts
only to feel
my voids and failures.
Keep me alive
this last hour
so I can speak of you
one more time.

YOU LEFT ME

You left me
without a word,
not even consolation
in this desperation.
I didn't know
that I must wait
for even a moment
of my regret.
Days and days
in darkness I can't see;
not a word
in this desolation.
I wait in silence
only to know
that in desperation
I might know.
Only your vision
remained in the night;
how can I arrive
to this upheld site?
Roads and roads
are traveled for you,
yet only a step
can I foresee.
My existence lacks,
my promises fail,
for your return
I wait in vain.
A dimming light
in the horizon
allows me hope
that I can shine.

IN THE RAIN YOU WALKED

You left alone
in the rain, you walked;
nothing, you said,
will appease your heart.
Redemption and Glory
are the tickets you bought,
nothing will make you forget
this right.
You left your fortune
and destiny
to find a way
better then me.
Through the streets you walked
until you felt the pain
all night you ran
until your sacrifice remained.
Remained, so you could vow
remained, so you could know
remained so you remember
your promises and oaths.

THE RIGHT

Your loneliness
gave you the right
to break
my trying heart.
Your desperation
gave you the strength
to undo
my desperate life.
Your broken state
gave you the talent
to toy
with my wanting soul.
Your disappointments
gave you the strength
to keep me
for another day.
Your deception
let you forget
that I might need
a little more.

ANOTHER DAY

Another day
on this long-winded train;
whose destiny
will be proclaimed?
I will wait
so you can rise
and fulfill
your awaited plan.
Even though
you left long ago,
your eyes
I still remember.
Many got on
this promised ride
only to be
forgotten.
Your stubbornness
made me wait
your adamant point of view
gave me strength.
On board again
for another journey,
perhaps this time
you'll make it through.
A forgiving hour
your luck may bring,
a hearing ear
you may summon.

YOU KNOW

You know the truth
about my life.
You know the truth
of my sacrifice.
I lost more
than you think I should.
I lost more
than you think I can conquer.
I have to hold
to that old promise,
even in this
trying time.
The letters and symbols
still protect me;
signs and oaths
are leading me on.
I will hold on to you
and your promise
the one you made
long ago.

TOO YOUNG

Your deliverance slipped away,
you were too young to wonder, still,
even then, you surpassed
my deepest doubt.
Have patience in this wanting hour,
believe that even this time
will uplift
your soul.
Your innocence still lives;
your eyes are as bright
even in
this cold night.
Your deliverance was endured
in the darkest hour
long after
it was over.
Forgive me;
forgive your chances
but rest assured—
your time will come.

DON'T BLAME ME

If you blame my name,
if you blame my promise,
if you don't let me go
I will pray to a higher ground;
A ground so lofty
and true
you won't even know
what came over you.
I am a prisoner
to your limitations,
a prisoner
to your hopes.
A prisoner,
my desires are trampled;
as a prisoner,
my yearnings are lost.
You will be judged;
every deed considered.
Let me go,
free my heart.
A prisoner,
for no reason,
my innocence
will lead the way.

TIRED SOULS

Tired souls,
forgetful minds,
weary hearts,
dazed lives.
The latest influences
and latest trends,
before dawn,
they do amend.
In this hour
we await
those
who can stay awake.
Who will serve?
Who will mourn?
This is the last time,
perhaps, to know.
I struggled for a century
for my right
not to die
on this night.

TOO FAR GONE

Too far gone,
your dreams did slip away;
too far gone
your glory is still remembered.
A moment of my time
is a lifetime for you.
You know yourself
that it will never be true.
You left me
the moment you saw my face,
you turned your back
on my deepest regret.
You lost time,
your fears were real;
you'll take away my chance
just to let you feel.
You buried the evidence,
even my pleas,
my supplication in vain
more then you can bear.
I will wait in the storm,
take comfort in the winds,
walk with nothing in sight
for another night.
Your loss is my
Prison;
your troubles
are my measure.

WIN OR LOSE

We wait in peace
in this forgetting hour;
we wait in peace
in these desperate times.
To heaven we look,
for forgiveness we cry;
our return will rectify
the burdens of time.
To heaven we look,
forforgiveness we cry;
in the eyes of God,
we attempt to try.
We wait in peace,
we wait in strength;
to stand strong
and wait in faith.
Win or lose
in this awaiting hour;
an angel hovers
in these desperate times.

THE STATUS

I hope for change;
I pray for transformation.
You want to smoothe the lines,
afraid of tribulations.
I want to grow
and expand;
you want it the same,
afraid it is not time.
I want to feel and
outgrow my limitations;
you want to appease,
afraid I will know.
I want to learn,
I want to find;
you want to cover
that the need is mine.
I believe there is peace,
I believe there is hope;
you are afraid to know,
afraid to cope.
The earth is red,
the waters blue,
the air is clear,
the fire hot.

CHANCES

I have room
for a helping hand.
I have a need
that still honors.
You have everything
before my time;
I have nothing
before yours.
I still need
when you see me;
my measure is right
my desire still true.
Your fortunes arrived
before my chances.
You still worry
about your right.
You will turn away
because you know of your losses,
you won't lend an ear
because you know of my right.
The light shines,
the colors glitter
on both of us
in this lowly night.
The dice was rolled,
the road was open
loyalties unfold
tonight.

IN VELVET ATTIRED

I saw your name,
I saw your light,
garbed in glory,
adorned in might.
In Velvet attired
in linens and lace,
silk and taffeta,
majestic in grace.
Understanding your reasons,
understanding your ways
beauty untold,
a mystifying face.
Forgetting our surety,
forgetting our pride,
your faith will carry
you through this night.
Called by your promise,
called by your oaths,
called by your vows,
you shine at your call.

YOUR GATES PREVAIL

Open to instruction,
open to the light,
open to your kingdom,
Your gates prevail.
Humble before you,
in awe and anticipation;
I wait in darkenkness
for your majesty.
Understanding greatness,
understanding truth,
understanding mercy
and nobility.

THE PERFECT SKY

The winds blow
in this dusty night;
the sun sets
in the perfect sky.
The blameless horizon
appears once again;
the bright stars
shine perfectly.
Will I sustain?
the glory of the night
or fall again
in desperation?
The earth is hot
from enduring the times;
the sun burns
through the feeble lines.
Will I live again?
Will I shine brightly?
If I am encouraged by your faith
and eternal lights.
At dusk
still waiting,
at nightfall,
still here.

THE ANGEL HOVERS

With the knife over my head
the angel hovers above me
Will your righteousness save me?
Will your glory suffice?.
As the darkness comes down
and the fog envelopes,
your clear air I still breathe,
your salvation I feel.
As the collectors knock,
as wickedness approaches,
your strength still prevails
your vows still hold.
As the oppressor takes over
and the losses comes for revenge,
your promises still hold;
your commandments are alive.
As the children scream,
as the workers moan,
your rays still shine through;
your oaths still save me.
As the people cry out,
as the women fall from hunger,
your hopes still sustain;
your prayers still keep.

AN EYE TO SEE

I have
an eye to see,
an ear to hear,
legs to walk upon
and arms to build.
I have
the sun to warm me,
the sea to cool me
the winds to blow
and the stars to shine upon me.
I have
a tree for shade,
a flower to beautify my senses,
rain to satiate,
and storms to mystify.
The earth turns
and we try a little harder;
the ground is hot;
the time has come.

THE FISH DO SWIM

In anger to advance
and innocence to hope
I digest the facts
for my fortunes to know.
The fish do swim
in fertile streams,
playfully awaiting
a savior to rise.
I converse in truth
While the fires do burn;
I wait in vain
yet the earth still turns.
To walk in peace,
my reflection I see,
I see for nothing,
my fertility.
I hear finally
of your tamed reality
I roar in vain
for a savior train.
I act foolishly
after waiting wholeheartedly
I use wisely;
in justice I weigh.

STONES AND GEMS

Wisdom and understanding
fortunes and fame
where is my luck?
my chances are twain.
Stones and gems
in glory sanctify;
luck and fortunes are
like the rays of the sun.
Justice and mercy,
which road to take?
I wait for your blessings
in this lonely state.
Shine down on me,
give me your signs,
let me feel
your merciful love.
You left your glory
in this shattered earth,
you left only remnants
of the dust of your world.
Give me your blessings
I await my fortunes,
not to err
in my virtue
I hope.
Blue,
red
white and yellow
an oracle
will show me your way.

THE ROAD

The road is paved
in stones and pebbles;
the road is paved
toward eternity.
The road once lost,
my dreams and visions;
the road once kept
my hopes and fears.
Some remained and some were forgotten
yet we still merge towards the night;
the road still holds their eternal promise
the road still hopes for their eternal light.
True is their right,
true is their sacrifice,
each one a symbol,
each one an enduring light.
I can still know
in this long surrender;
I can still catch
a glimpse of their might.
Let us awaken and be inspired
Let us revive and recall
pillars and statues
from the ages.
Stones and gems
will adorn eternity,
Dressed in gold and blue velvet
each one right, each one garbed.
Diamonds and sapphires,
rubies and emeralds,
adorn their armor
for eternal bravery.

Lyres and drums,
harps and violins,
trumpets and flutes,
will lead the way.
Twelve stood for honor;
twelve was their glory
their road was paved
on the highways of long ago.
Their roads still await
in the same measure.
Their road still calls
to those who long.

THE CALL OF MY HEART

The sound of trumpets
the call of my heart
leading the way and
announcing possibility.
The sound of triumph is
the summoning of the hopes,
the calling of the people that
shows them the way.
The song that is in my heart
still plays awaiting;
the life that is deep in my soul
still manifests in anticipation.
A stream flows constantly;
I can almost hear
that eternal
calling.

BRIGHT AS THE LIGHT OF THE HEAVENS

Bright as the light of the stars
reflecting the glory of the heavens,
blessed under the light of the moon
their faces shine as on their wedding day.
Hoping faithfully,
waiting whole-heartedly,
standing bravely,
under the canopy.
Under the skies
their faces are bright;
under the heavens
their bodies are strong.
Faithfully awaiting
their vows and promises,
they are willfully mirroring
an eternal call.

THE YELLOW SUN

The brown earth
and yellow sun,
the blue seas
and red ground.
will remind me of another day;
and awaken my heart,
inspire my soul
until your return.
The gray sky and
the stormy clouds,
the blizzard in the heart of winter,
the rain on a summer's day.
Will lead me on, so I can conquer,
they will waken my sleepy heart
will bring back me back to existence
and carry me for another day.
Your ancient promise,
your call from long ago,
your enduring light,
and everlasting plight
will forgive my wounded life,
will return my broken shores
will summon my long ago promise
and inspire my rising sign.

MY RIGHT HAND RAISED

My right hand is raised,
my right leg first
my heart is wanting
my mind is clear.
Actions,
responses,
receptivity,
suggestion.
My eyes open,
my ears listen,
my nose smells
my hair shines.
Vision,
discrimination,
senses,
realization.
The rainbow is colorful,
the sky is blue,
the lions roar,
the kings judge.
Waiting,
seeing,
expressing,
thinking.
Reflecting on the shining moon,
understanding the rays from above;
thinking about reality,
concluding my state of existence.
Intuition,
meaning,
stability,
bondage.

The tower collapses,
the skies thunder,
the earth shakes,
in wisdom I await.

REGENERATION

Regeneration from an old existence
I outgrow any reminder of apathy,
a revelation of a higher reality
I transcend once more.
Awaken into a new state
My vows are once again renewed
transforming my failures
into the light of the day.
A response in due season
shows the power of suggestion,
offers a receptive face to see
in the darkness of times.
Stability in these times of hardship
will raise a discriminating heart.
Intuition as cool as water
will lift my heart.

CONTEND

Contend with ideals,
contend with perfection,
contend with reality,
realize what is true.
Feel the hurt,
forget the blame,
feel the injustice,
live the pain.
Live your life,
achieve your success,
your potential reach
hopes to overcome.

ONE IS MERIT

One is merit,
one is claime
one decides
between.
One confuses,
one covers up,
one attempts,
to forget the night.
One knows,
one tries,
one summons
the only chance.
One recalls,
one acts,
God decides,
which shall know.

AN OPEN HAND

An open hand
for an awaiting soul
a grateful man
waiting and pleading.
A house built
thoughtfully by
a toiling man
who in his hopes awaits.
A sword
drawn properly
by a brave warrior
in anticipation.
Water bestowed
on a thirsty being who
awaits
eagerly.
These doors open
these gates to the worlds beyond;
thoughtfully
we await.
A chariot rides
across the cusps of heaven
while quietly the riders
transcend.

ONE

One merits,
one demands;
the finger of God
decides between them.
One kneels down,
one stands tall;
the finger of God
chooses the victor.
One cries,
one proclaims;
the finger of God
points toward the right.
One gives,
one takes away;
the finger of God
decides.
One manifests,
one hides;
the finger of God
chooses.
One gathers,
one scatters;
the finger of God
points.
One demands,
one implores;
the finger of God
decides.

GOD WILL GUIDE

Pleasure and answer,
ecstasy and despair,
war and peace,
who will repair?
God will guide
in perfect balance;
God will show
in perfect truth.
Tranquility and strife
we can decipher;
stability and relief
who will find?
God will know,
God will answer,
God will keep
the humble man.
A slave
a prisoner
in a helpless existence,
free to toil
for another day.

BEAUTY A DAY

Foundation is wisdom,
peace is God;
beauty is a day
in the week of the soul.
Wealth and poverty,
seed and deprivation,
life and death,
sovrereignity and desolation.
The wage of peace
is war at times,
the wage of honor,
in shame in some.
Beauty a day,
ugliness an answer
peace can win
if all can answer.
To weigh,
to measure,
to mine,
to dig,
a seed,
a life,
a kingdom to reap.
North
south
west and east
foundations in a kingdom
will be conquered and won.

THE RAM ASKED FIRST

The ram jumped first,
pioneered the unventured land;
the ram thought first
venturing the unworked ground.
The ram asked first
the never-answered question;
the ram pointed
to the untraveled road.
The ram offered
the precious oil of anointment;
the ram gave its horns
for proclamation.

FIRE FROM WATER

Fire from water
And blame from innocence,
loss from the kingdom,
destruction from wholeness.
Winds blow,
storms thunder,
angels minister,
God reins.
Water from air,
luminosity from the moon,
light from the sun,
reflection from water.
The gates await,
the doors open,
the skies prevail,
the voices resound.
God directs
God will center.
One truth
carries all.

THE SUN IS HOT

The sun is hot
in these hard times;
give me shade
so I can think.
Another day
I will ask for,
so I can mend
my irreconcilable state.
The moon cools
the scorching times,
inspiring us,
and our imaginations.
Another night
brings me shade
helps me mourn
my desolation.
The freezing rain
in the cold morn,
the falling snow
will appease my existence.
Another season
passed by
perhaps tomorrow
you will know.
Hail, rain,
snow and sun,
water cools
my thirsty soul.

AN EAR TO HEAR

I have this ear to hear,
an eye to see
and arms to reach
my eternity.
I have this brow to raise,
a nose to smell,
and a mouth to speak
of your forever.
I have this stomach to digest,
These teeth to chew,
And a finger to point
to the ways of truth.
I have this will to attest,
a mind to remember
this heart to implore
for my fruitfulness, and prosperity.

THE HIGHWAY WINDS

The highway winds,
echoe tonight
the journeys lights
flicker.
My heart's desires
awaken in wonder,
my body's aches
warm the street.
Danger, urgency and desperation
enliven the mighty
flimsy despair,
deaden the hopes.
Forget the times
when you were not;
forget my life
for another day.
At a single point
I do focus.
Like the flame of a candle
I stand.

RED CRIED

Red cried,
yellow wept,
blue remembered,
and white kept.
Dancing, shining
their lights reflect
a fortune,
a name
of beauty and grace.
The last night
before forever;
the last night
before the splendor.
Day before eternity
passing eludes the restless.
The last before the dawn,
forever I do keep.
The longest night,
the longest hour,
before the sun
rises.
Red cried,
yellow wept,
blue remembered,
and white kept.

WILL MAKE A MARK

I will make a mark
that will endure the trends;
will make a stamp
that will shake the times.
One night will last
one night will change;
faith will sign
the Eternal name.
The tides will shift,
the land will rock,
the waves will break,
and change the lights.

WATCHING OVER YOU

One God up in the heaven
faithful and true;
one God up in the heaven
watching over you.
Signs govern
the days that guide
the elements that rule
over our times.
Look and listen while you can,
placed under the sun on this earth
One God under the heavens
lets us know.

LUCK AND FORTUNE

Luck and fortune,
good wishes and fame,
life and blessings
without a name.
Simplicity and straightness,
intention and reality;
meaning;
in an only truth.
Inheritance and faith
are the venues left
what you truly deserve
is where your heart mends.
My soul wants
only for a moment.
The best of the good
is what I desire.
The sun shines,
the moon reflects
a yearning being
you will bless.

SO I STAND ALONE

So I stand alone,
so you stand strong;
in between us
is a narrow path.
a narrow path.
My senses are numb
on this narrow path;
silence lies,
narrow path,
narrow spaces,
narrow passages,
in between.
Nothing better
that my eyes can see,
tied together,
in surety.

TRUST

Trust your senses,
trust your name,
trust your lights,
hearts do mend.
Think about a matter;
weigh the truth within;
transform your only chance
into a worthy reality.
Move, see, and act,
believe, hope and feel;
the last say is God's
for eternitiy
On His throne he does reign
abundant mercy and faithfulness
he awaits to bestow,
forever crowned in centeredness.

IN THE FAR AWAKENING

In the far awakening
of my soul
I caught a glimpse
of your legacy.
In the rooms and halls
of my existence
I felt the touch
of your hopes.
In the faraway desires
of my waking dreams
I breathed the air
of your burning life.
In the faraway answers
of my hopeful mind
I heard the sound
of your beating heart.
Will you make it back?
after this destruction
will you return?
after feeling the pain.

I DIDN'T SAY A WORD

I didn't say a word,
I didn't betray your trust;
you thought I would scream
and take away your right.
I didn't say a word
I was awake this time;
I understood the meaning
of all that was mine.
I didn't say a word
I stayed awake all night;
I didn't tell on you
didn't give away your chance.

A PULSE

A pulse;
life signs
weakly appear
in this desolate land.
Whirlwinds and storms
Await a return
after this long run
suggestions do mourn.
Steps light paths,
steps leading the way
legs pioneer roads,
legs support the stay.
Yellow as the sun,
white as the moon,
reflections in the waters
will illuminate wonder.
The shades of the night
highlight perpetually,
the spectre of chance
reappears slowly.
The rainbow of revelation
comes through,
the myriads of instruction
teaches carefully.

MERIT

Merit, will know,
merit will toil,
merit will ask,
merit will choose.
Mercy will plead,
mercy will bestow,
mercy will forgive,
mercy will know.
Desired as a rose,
desired as the morning dew,
desired as the summer day,
desired as love.
Blame will take away,
blame will deprive,
blame will forget,
blame will scatter.
Honesty will tell,
honesty will open up,
honesty will fall apart,
honesty will break your heart.

A SACRIFICE MADE

A sacrifice made
will last forever;
once faithful,
always true.
In the moment of uncertainty
you stood your ground;
in the moment of answers
you did come through.
A sacrifice made,
strong always,
once faithful,
forever the same.
When the walls came down,
uncertainty failed,
when the world shattered,
only surety prevailed.
A covenant, an oath
will strengthen my bones;
a promise, a vow
will come through when I am hurt.

I'LL TELL YOU TOO MUCH

I'll tell you too much
if I get to know you;
I'll tell you too much
if I adore.
I'll suffer
for you;
I'll wait,
if you try.
I'll tell you too much
if I just follow;
I'll tell I too much
if I show my love.

IT IS MERCY

It is not forgiveness
but mercy;
it is not honesty
but truth;
It is not justice
just choice;
it is not guilt
but reality.
Justice for all.
Choices are here,
truth unravels
for all to see.
It's forgiveness of the almighty,
it's mercy of the creator.
He is that which He is;
there is no other.

WAITING

Waiting,
listening,
hoping,
yearning.
Waiting too long
can cause heartache;
bury my heart
if I forget.
Reflecting,
Understanding,
thinking,
concluding.
Reflecting on the moon
can awaken suggestion;
wake me up
if I am dreaming.
The tower falls,
the skies thunder,
the earth shakes,
for my coming fate.

MEANING

The power of meaning
the realization of truth
the reversal of fortune
the discrimination of lies.
Away from bondage,
away from toil,
away from oppression,
away from cries.
The transformation of the ages,
the regeneration of the soul,
and the awakening of hearts
are suggestions that mourn.
I move toward stability,
toward liberty,
toward receptivity,
toward redemption.

READY TO BE MOLDED

The clay
is ready to be molded
the mortar
is ready to be formed.
From nothing
he built;
from void
there was something.
He supported,
he formed,
he anointed;
snow to dust.
An even life force
ebbs urgently,
last hopes
are actualized.

THE MINISTERING ANGELS

The ministering angels
and the reigning winds
establish the throne
and guard its foundation.
The source of His glory,
the source of His fame
is a fortress from days of old,
an establishment for the ages.
Twelve leaders of the soul,
twelve months of the year,
twelve lucks in the heavens,
seven are the stars.
All the speaking tongues
and all forms of creation
were born from nothing
into a vast potential.
Beams were created to support
and pillars of winds to uphold
the ground was mined
and anointed.
The angels decided on the letters
they faced in all directions
the spirit of God,
out of void.

WEARY

Weary of the night,
weary of the fight,
weary of the battle,
afraid of the rights.
People look,
people answer,
people play,
taking chances.
The world turns,
the world runs,
to win the race
and keep up with my times.

HE WAITED

He waited
when he formed
and conceived the whole
without diminishing.
He waited
when he formed
for the eternal mercy
of the creator.
He slept
when they knew,
never losing a moment
of his eternal faith.

ALONG THE TOWER

All along the tower
the guards do stand,
surrounding the fortress
that was built in my heart.
In the distance
freedom winks an eye,
reaching the skies
that will let me hope.
Stability and strength
gives assurance
Is it real?
Is it true?
The guards are alerted
watching the towers,
moving the night
into another day.
The arms and swords
glean in preparation;
will they deflect
the enemy's advance?
Guarding the night,
protecting the masses,
hoping to reflect
stability.

LOOK AROUND

People look around
and point fingers
to the chosen and
to those who forego.
Blame and derision
point the way;
coherence and understanding
defer the cost.
The loss of lives,
the cost of a kingdom,
only virtue can win
this war.
The love of wisdom,
the love of honor,
the desire for justice
will defray.
Defray the cost of lust,
the cost of jealousy
God's sovereignity
like morning dew.
Rain on me,
rain on the injustice.
Shine on my existence,
heal the souls.
Some in vain
some for a reason
give me shelter
so I can hide.
Hide me from wrong,
hide me from fear,
hide me from my oppressors
that want my soul.

THE CHILD

The gun in the child's hand
Is waiting to be fired;
let me lie
on this minefield,
absorb the bombs,
absorb the lashes,
tomorrow I will wake
as though unharmed.
Hoping to deflect
this broken justice,
I take the arrows
of cruelty.
A boy points his gun
in my direction;
let me walk away
as nothing.
Forgive the children.
Who can judge?
All sides look around.
Who can hide?

STORMS

Storms and fair-weather,
difficulty and pain
will tomorrow come?
without a name.
On a tightrope
my legs shake;
quicksand and minefields
show me the way.
Shaking from the cold
and hard spoken lines
I try to subdue
my unborn love.
Watching my steps
bullets sound in the distance;
bring back the plow
so we can build again.
A new morn
smartened by the storm;
a new beginning
shakes to last.
Bless me from above,
shelter me,
give me mercy;
in Your glory I want to be.

DECORATED

Decorated with velvet
curtains tied in ropes;
all your worldly possessions
are displayed on the walls.
In your mind you will pass,
Another day will appease you
but in the whole, who will judge?
Only the righteous.
Your conquests
and trophies
will let you pass andother day,
you will leave an impression.
But who will know?
the victor;
the knight;
only the almighty.

A PRAYER

To thrive on weakeness
is a living sin;
to exist because of my suffering
is what you mean.
A prayer,
a hope,
a psalm,
from above.
Conspiracy will help you.
You will prey on my failures
and that is wrong,
if that is all,
My ending is sad.
in your eyes;
let me leave
for another.

LEAVING

Leaving is my only response
leaving what I believe in
was the only answer,
my only chance.
To understand and to know
are the only reasons
that can only be given
to higher rights.
They sabotaged
the only answers,
they were jealous
of the true light.
They bombed your light,
destroyed the answers
so you never know
what was right.
They killed, they wounded;
their only solutions
turned out the lights
in obscurity scurried.
They covered their steps
for they did falter;
the moment came
and they let it pass.
They lost their moment
forever covering,
even to kill
a living light.

TONIGHT I LEAVE

Tonight I leave
undecided;
did I help you a little?
did I do right?
I left you as helpless
as your desires
empty and lost
as I knew.
Look around you
What do you think?
Can you be beautiful
and grow once more?

FOGGY NIGHT

Those eternal lights
have dimmed tonight,
too vague to decipher
in this foggy night.
My bones are weakened
after the storm;
my light faded
after my loss.
Not to err,
I do beseech you
let me stand
and meet your right.
Where my gift lies
is too hard to realize.
Who will know
the impressions of true reality?
To reach, I hope
in vain to see
your glorious call
is something to me.
My feeble lines
perhaps will reach you,
to know the truth
about my hopes.
Tonight I leave
any freedom costly;
I can't bear
your only right.
I'll try once more
to listen closely
I will try once more
to feel your heart.

NOT TOO HARD

To swat my existence,
to kill my chance
is not too hard
in these desperate times.
To blame, to wound
a living person,
is too easy
in these forgetful nights.
Giving me away
is all but common
an everyday happening
in these lands.
Common ground,
common answers,
have become the mighty god
of honest men.
Mediocrity rules,
mediocrity reins,
struck by lightening
slapped tonight.
A wanderer,
a wounded spirit,
can I teach you love?
in these forgetfull times.

A FADING DREAM

A fading vision,
a fading dream;
can still inspire,
can still mean.
Even after
a shattering
even after
a breaking.
A distant light,
will lead me again;
A distant knight
I will not forgo.
The bells
toll;
the world still turns;
unto another return.

Printed in the United States
40169LVS00002B/46